THE PRICE OF GREATNESS

Bishop Nicholas Duncan-Williams

The Price of Greatness

All rights reserved. No part of this publication may be reproduced, stored in a retrieval system, or transmitted, in any form or by any means, electronic, mechanical, photocopying, recording, or otherwise without written permission from the author or publisher.

Copyright 1998, Nicholas Duncan-Williams

ISBN 1-56229-199-8

Pneuma Life Publishing, Inc.
4451 Parliament Place
Lanham, Maryland 20706
301-577-4052
http://www.pneumalife.com

Printed in the United States of America
   1 3 5 7 9 10 8 6 4 2

Contents

Introduction

Chapter 1	The Purpose Of Greatness	9
Chapter 2	Mentors/Point Of Reference	13
Chapter 3	The Test Of Greatness	23
Chapter 4	Building Lasting Relationships	29
Chapter 5	Concerning Your Rights	31
Chapter 6	Honor To Whom Honor Is Due	37
Chapter 7	Unlimited Greatness	43
Chapter 8	The Challenges Of Greatness	47
Chapter 9	Preserving Greatness	51
Chapter 10	Ebenezer	55

Introduction

TRUE GREATNESS

The lust for power, money and sex has dominated our world since time immemorial. This lust has often generated unhealthy competitions amongst friends, families and co-laborers of Christ. People sacrifice one another in any form in order to attain what they desire.

It is commonly believed that anyone who possesses more power and money is great. Jesus however, said that a man's life does not consist of the abundance of things he possesses (Luke 12:15). John the Baptist possessed no earthly goods and yet Jesus described him as the greatest man of his day (Matt. 11:11).

Our values as Christians have changed so much that sometimes we get confused about how to set our priorities right. When I received the call into ministry decades ago, greatness was not the issue at stake. Obedience and faithfulness to one's call was what mattered most.

Fame, financial prosperity and influence may come

The Price of Greatness

with greatness, but we must realize that handling these successfully is more difficult than obtaining them.

Greatness comes from God. He told Abraham that He would make his name great. God confers greatness on people through His own sovereign act. Two people may possess the same wealth and exert the same authority and yet one would be greater than the other.

The disciples of Jesus once asked Him of the greatest person in the kingdom of God. Jesus answered the question in a most fascinating manner. He called a little child unto Him and set him in the midst of them. He then stated that unless one is converted and becomes like a little child, one cannot enter the kingdom of God (Matt. 18:1). Jesus in other words was describing greatness as follows:

1) God must establish the great man. Jesus set the child in the midst of the people. Don't seek to establish yourself in your own strength and wisdom.

2) Jesus associated greatness with conversion. A change of heart, change of life, change of motives and a change of attitude is the beginning of greatness.

3) Thirdly, Jesus spoke about greatness within the context of the kingdom of God. Greatness can only be attained through kingdom principles and it must be dedicated to the promotion of God's kingdom.

Introduction

There is a way to know if your greatness comes from God. Greatness, which comes from God, returns to Him. That kind of greatness submits to God and also channels all its benefits into the kingdom of God. The greatness of the world is however, squandered in the pleasures of this world.

This book seeks to lead you along the paths of true greatness. You'll discover how to receive greatness and give glory to God with it.

Chapter 1

THE PURPOSE OF GREATNESS

The purpose of greatness is to give others a raise. Don't ever use your greatness to suppress other people. A man can be so busy chasing after greatness that he has no time to help anyone else. It is very easy to be addicted to greatness. The fear of losing it keeps people bound to things one must do in order to remain great.

When one assumes a status of greatness one must continually make plans to seek people who can be raised with ones greatness. The opposite is often the case; we seek whom we can control with our greatness.

David, after being persecuted by Saul for years, finally ascended unto the throne as king of Israel. It was natural for Him to have harassed the family of Saul who was dead. He however, began to seek a member of Saul's family whom he could use his greatness to help.

'And the king said, Is there not yet any of the house of Saul, that I may shew the kindness of God unto him? And Ziba said unto the king, Jonathan hath yet a son, which is lame on his feet.

Now when Mephibosheth, the son of Jonathan, the son of Saul, was come unto David, he fell on his face, and did reverence. And David said, Mephibosheth. And he answered, Behold thy servant!

And David said unto him, Fear not: for I will surely shew thee kindness for Jonathan thy father's sake, and will restore thee all the land of Saul thy father; and thou shalt eat bread at my table continually.' I Sam. 9:3, 6, 7

David sought someone he could bless. Most people would have sought to eliminate every family member of Saul for fear that these family members might undermine their leadership.

True greatness never feels insecure. Greatness must be used as a tool to enhance the development of other people; it must not be used as a lethal weapon to destroy others. David was kind to Mephibosheth. He restored his fathers' land to him and gave him the right hand of fellowship.

In order for greatness to be a blessing to people, it must seek others. The weak and needy must not come knocking on our doors for help; we must seek them and raise them up.

Greatness must be transparent enough and approachable enough for others to benefit from. David

Purpose of Greatness

shared his table with Mephibosheth. Sometimes our success is shrouded in mystery so much so that instead of encouraging others it rather discourages them.

Most successful people would readily show you their strengths but not their weakness. You never see their moments of fear and anxiety. This makes it impossible for you to accomplish much because you quickly condemn yourself and give up when moments of fear come.

You don't know that great people experience exactly what you experience. The difference is that they have learned to move on in spite of their fears. Elijah, the great "fire-prophet" had his moments of fear.

'Elias was a man subject to like passions as we are, and he prayed earnestly that it might not rain and it rained not on the earth by the space of three years and six months.' James 5:17

You must not tell your followers all your failures and weaknesses all the time but it is also wrong to hide everything from them.

There are many uncomfortable things one is likely to go through when you want to help others with your greatness. Some of the people really don't want to be helped. They make no personal effort to rise. They're content with the crumbs from the table.

There may be others who have bad attitudes and character traits that will wage war against every input you make in them. Elisha could not help Gehazi. Gehazi preferred being a thief to being a chief. He preferred being a liar to being a leader.

The Price of Greatness

The great man may also come across people who are not satisfied with anything less than what the great man has. They will use every foul means to have your level of recognition, your measure of grace, your level of breakthrough and even your dimension of spiritual gifts.

In spite of these problems, a great man must make his greatness available. John the Baptist stood the risk of losing his following and yet he introduced Jesus as being greater than himself. He said Jesus must increase, but I must decrease.

This position of John the Baptist did not hinder him from being great. Jesus Christ later asserted that John the Baptist was greater than all men born in his time. Do not ever forget, that God will make a man great in order for him to become a blessing to the world around him.

Chapter 2

Mentors/Point Of Reference

We know that God is the source of all true greatness. Nevertheless, He makes arrangements through which great men are released.

It is very interesting to hear people say that they received Christ all by themselves; others also say that they received the Holy Ghost baptism all by themselves - no one laid hands on them. There is yet another group of people who insist that they have no mentors in the ministry. Nobody trained them. The Holy Ghost trained them.

People say these things to add to the power of their testimonies. I don't dispute that such direct encounters between God and men do exist. Nevertheless, such experiences are not superior to instances where God used men to raise and to reach other men.

Peter was invited by his brother Andrew to meet Jesus, yet he was the leader of the apostles. Elijah raised Elisha and yet the former had the double portion anointing.

'Iron sharpeneth iron; so a man sharpeneth the countenance of his friend.' Prov. 27:17

Every great man must have a human point of reference (mentor). When the Samaritan woman asked Jesus for the water which satisfies, Jesus asked her to go and bring her husband. Jesus wanted a point of reference.

'Jesus saith unto her, Go call thy husband, and come hither.' John 4:16

There are heights in the things of God you cannot attain unless you have a point of reference. Lone rangers don't last in the things of God. The point of reference could be the one who led us to Christ, someone who laid hands on us to receive the Holy Spirit baptism, someone who taught us in Sunday school or someone who introduced us into the ministry and trained us. God will not directly do all these things in the life of a person without the use of a human instrument.

One cannot have a point of reference by reading a book, by watching videotape, or by listening to an audiotape. It has to be through physical contact and intimacy.

I have never failed to keep my humble beginnings in proper perspective. Beloved, I owe it all to the Lord Jesus Christ. He is the one who makes all the differ-

Mentors / Point of Reference

ence in my life. I have never forgotten the circumstances through which I lost my three fingers, and my close shave with death. I have never forgotten how God used an Indian woman by the name of Mrs. Rajj to preach the gospel of Jesus Christ to me. I have never forgotten how God used the Acquah sisters, at the Korle Bu Teaching Hospital to invite me to the Church of Pentecost where I graciously received the baptism of the Holy Ghost. Beloved, I have never forgotten how I used to walk several kilometers every day to church and back. There are several points of references in my life, and each time I think about them, it reminds me of how faithful God is.

None of us knows what the future holds, but we can call upon God for His direction into the future. We all have plans and purposes under the sun that we desire to attain. To attain greatness, we have to experience more or less what the great men of old like, Moses, Joseph, Isaac, David, Daniel, Job, Peter and Paul, experienced. We have to be tried and tested. One has to go through the wilderness experience and succeed to have a point of reference. Remember, if others have made it, so can you. God will not directly do all these things without the use of a human instrument.

Through men like Archbishop Bishop Benson Idahosa of blessed memory, I obtained a scholarship to attend Bible School in Benin City, Nigeria. Through Archbishop Benson Idahosa, my life in ministry was streamlined. Through him, God opened great doors of ministry to me worldwide. Today, by the grace of God, I have ministered, and I am still ministering to countless numbers of people across the continents of the world, bringing them the good news that Jesus saves.

Paul, the apostle, had a spectacular encounter with Jesus in his conversion to the Lord. This not withstanding, Jesus did not lay hands on him to receive the Holy Ghost. Jesus used Ananias to do this. Again the Holy Spirit used Barnabas to introduce Paul to the believers in Jerusalem. It is worth noting that John the Baptist was the point of reference of Jesus. No matter how great one is, one cannot introduce himself to the world. This is the proper way to do it.

> '*And Jesus answering said unto him, suffer it to be so now: for thus it becometh us to fulfill all righteousness. Then he suffered him.*'   Matt. 2:15

To have a point of reference is not only proper but it is also righteous. It is proper because that is the only way by which one can really prosper. It is righteous because it is the only way by which we can remain successful.

Having a point of reference is not a disincentive to ministry but an incentive. It is easier to build upon the hard earned reputation, integrity and testimony of a proven minister or ministry, than to struggle on our own to make an impression. A positive word of testimony from some proven ministers can open doors for us easily. What a minister may struggle to attain in ten years could be attained in just one year if he uses his point of reference well.

The point of reference is also important because it defines a certain code of ethics for us to operate within. The Apostle Paul drew the attention of the Philippian believers to the need to follow the pattern set by the point of reference.

'Those things which ye have both learned, and received, and heard, and seen in me, do; and the God of peace shall be with you.'   Phil. 4:9

The God of peace will be with you if you have learned, received, heard and seen the right things in the sight of God. This means that having a point of reference is more than carrying a membership or ordination certificate around. If a man hangs loosely and carelessly around a great minister or ministry and learns nothing, he has no point of reference.

Those who are privileged by God to be a point of reference, must also be careful about what they pass on to their followers in terms of teaching and conduct. To be a point of reference is no easy matter. The judgment of God on the point of reference is greater than that of the student.

'My brethren, be not many masters, knowing that we shall receive the greater condemnation.'   James 3:1

Points of reference don't only teach people what to do; they also teach people how to live. It is easy to go astray when one has no point of reference. If people know your roots they will readily see when you're going astray because they have a yardstick with which to measure you. Someone can easily point out to you that, what you receive practicing is not the practice of the main stream you flow out of.

The Price of Greatness

If people cannot trace where you came from, they cannot predict where you're going either. This explains why people who appear to be successful suddenly vanish in the same manner.

Having a point of reference protects us from attacks because we always have people to stand with us. The things, which are out there to destroy us, are many. The support of our contemporaries is not enough to protect us. We did not come out of our friends. They are therefore not likely to be passionately committed to our course. Our point of reference birthed us and will for that matter stand with us in times of trouble. Our point of reference gives testimony to what God has been able to do in our lives.

Jesus was born in a manger, a place so undignified for the Son of God, yet this did not change who He was or what He came to the world to do. Joseph came from slavery, through the prison, to the palace, and yet he did not let his attainment in life cloud his judgment for him to forget about his point of reference and his God who had delivered him and set him where he was. David rose from being a shepherd boy in the bush tendering his father's sheep to become the king of Israel.

Beloved, to claim to be a point of reference and not be around to defend and care for your seed is also gross irresponsibility. You must understand that it is your God-given right to have a point of reference amongst the numerous great ministries in the world. Any root God gives is His act of grace. You must receive it with thanksgiving.

Mentors / Point of Reference

'And of his fullness have all we received, and grace for grace.'   John 1:16

We must be careful never to undermine or be ungrateful to our point of reference. I remember an incident years ago, when I fell out with Archbishop Benson Idahosa of blessed memory, a man whom I owe so much in ministry. For a couple of years I felt I had arrived. Doors of opportunity were opening to me. I could perceive that the future was bright. I felt I was making it without the help of the Archbishop. What even kept me going in this direction was the fact that the some of my colleagues and I at the time, were of the opinion that we had nothing to do with this great man of God. We were self-made. The truth was that my colleagues didn't understand him, neither did they know him intimately, nor did they want to be associated with him. The opinion at the time was that, an association with this man of God meant that one was going to receive an impartation of his anointing as well as his weakness. Their opinions were projected to me, and in order to be in the good books of men, I bought it.

I was wrong. If this opinion were to be true, then the great men of God in the scriptures would have imparted to the recipients of their mantles, both their strengths and weakness. What was imparted was the gift of God, which passed through a human instrument not the weakness of men.

Beloved, Moses laid hands on Joshua in Deuteronomy 34:9, and the spirit of wisdom came upon him to lead Israel into the Promised Land.

Moses saw the Promised Land, but didn't enter it, had his weakness been transferred to Joshua by association and the laying on of hands, it would have been a different story altogether. The full account of Joshua's exploits, and how the Lord used him, can be read in the book of Joshua. Joshua's point of reference was Moses.

Elijah the Tishbite, was the point of reference for Elisha, son of Shaphat. He inherited a double portion of Elijah's anointing, and not his weaknesses.

Beloved, Timothy's point of reference was Paul the apostle. Who is your point of reference? Who are you? Who begat you? Are you self-made and thus have no point of reference? Be careful! You cannot be a point of reference if you don't have a point of reference.

As I earlier said, at the time, I received blessing from many quarters, not withstanding, I passed through the most difficult time as a minister of the Word of God. By the time I realized how unwise I was, a lot of things had gone wrong for me. I patched up with the Archbishop, and in no time I had this revelation that one must never undermine or be ungrateful to his or her point of reference.

It is biblical for us also to be a blessing to our points of reference by way of prayer, ministry and even material gifts. Those who sow spiritual things into our lives deserve to reap physical things from us (Romans 15:27). If you can catch this revelation, the blessings you can walk in, is unimaginable. For Timothy, Paul's blessing was, 'May God our Father and Jesus Christ our Lord show you kindness and mercy and give you great peace of heart and mind.' May this also, be your portion as you seek to honor your point of reference.

Chapter 3

THE TEST OF GREATNESS

The world assesses a man's greatness by the wealth he possesses and the power he wields. Earthly goods may accompany greatness but they don't by themselves prove greatness.

The test of a man's greatness is not in how much wealth and power he possesses but in how much temptations and trials he can endure.

Our Lord Jesus is the perfect example of greatness. His greatness is plainly attributed to His power of endurance. We are supposed to follow His example. Achievements will be subjected to severe test and if one has no endurance, all that he has built will crumble.

> *'Wherefore seeing we also are compassed about with so great a cloud of witnesses, let us lay aside every weight, and the sin which doth so easily beset us, and let us run with patience the race that is set before us,*

The Price of Greatness

Looking unto Jesus the author and finisher of our faith; who for the joy that was set before him endured the cross, despising the shame, and is set down at the right hand of the throne of God.'   Heb. 12:1, 2

We can only conclude that someone is great when he finishes his course successfully. To finish ones course however, requires great endurance. Jesus, though the Son of God, learned obedience through the many things He suffered. We cannot escape the need for endurance. Moses, the great leader, could not avoid the endurance element.

'By faith he forsook Egypt, not fearing the wrath of the king: for he endured, as seeing him who is invisible.' Heb.11: 27

The ultimate end of a great man is to see Jesus at the resurrection of the dead. To gain the world and lose one's soul is vanity.

Jesus talked about two men who built houses. One built his house upon a rock and the other built his upon the sand. Both builders obviously finished building. They both appeared great. Both projects appeared successful until the moment of test came. The Bible says that 'the rain descended, and the floods came, and the winds blew, and beat upon the houses.' The houses were subjected to severe test.

The house, which was built upon the rock, did not collapse because it was built upon the rock. The other house fell because it was built upon the sand.

Let us analyze the situation briefly. The one who built upon the rock was likely to have made slower

The Test of Greatness

progress. He had to work harder. He had to spend a lot of money breaking the rock at various points in order to make way for the foundation. Someone who intends to build upon a rock also requires the professional assistance of engineers and architects. There's no short cut in a situation when one has to build upon a rock.

Achievements are always subjected to tests. Unforeseen circumstances often come against what we have worked for within the space of many years. If we do not build according to biblically sound principles, our works will collapse.

It is wrong to attain greatness at the expense of another person. There are many ambitious people in the kingdom who will sacrifice their friends and brothers in the Lord in order to gain the advantage.

It is not wise to claim greatness when one has not been tested. You will soon realize that it is not easy to sustain, maintain and retain greatness, as it is to just acquire things.

'And the king of Israel answered and said, Tell him, Let not him that girdeth on his harness boast himself as he that putteth it off.' I Kings 70:11

The harness means the armor. One who is about to go to war must not boast as if he has been to the battlefield and won a war.

Human authorities will fight against a great man. Circumstances will seek to disappoint him. The devil will bring everything he has against people who are achieving. What would you do about accusation,

The Price of Greatness

blackmail, undermining, jealousy and rejection especially from people you consider close to you? People will criticize what the great man does out of jealousy and at the same time seek to do the same things. Opposition will necessarily come against a great man, because not many people like changes in their lives and environment. Great people are devoted to charting new paths and establishing fresh ways of thinking. Because they will not conform they are always being confronted. I have been misunderstood several times. I have endured many things through prayer. Greatness does not come to just anybody. Only people who are prepared to go the full distance can attain greatness.

Abraham Lincoln, the great U.S. Republican statesman, the 16th president of the United States of America, whose fame rests on his success in saving the Union in the Civil War and on his emancipation of slaves, was not ashamed of his humble beginnings, neither did he let his identity stifle his desire to succeed in life. He passed through the mill, to pay the price to become one of history's greatest men.

At age twenty-two, he set up a business, but it failed. When he was twenty-three, he ran for legislature and was defeated. Two years after failing to set up a business he tried again to set up another business, and it also failed. He did not let it become a stumbling block to his desire to succeed. At age twenty-five, two years after being defeated in his run for legislature, he tried again and this time was elected. At twenty-six, when he began to come into the limelight, he lost his sweet heart with whom he was going to share his success to

The Test of Greatness

the legislature. He had a nervous breakdown by the age of twenty-seven. When he was thirty-four years old, he ran for congress and failed. Three years later, he tried again and succeeded. After serving for two years he sought for re-election, but was defeated. At age forty-six he set his eyes on the senate and in his bid to get elected, he was defeated. He was not deterred. The following year, he run for a higher office, the office of the vice president, and was also defeated. At fifty-one, he run for the presidency, and was elected to become the greatest president of the United States of America.

What am I talking about? I am trying to get you to understand, that to attain greatness in life, you will be tested. If you try and fail, that is not the end of the world. You never know what you can do till you try; if at first you don't succeed, try, try, and try again.

Chapter 4

Building Lasting Relationships

Building of relationships is one of the last things most people who seek greatness consider important. We are often too busy trying to be the first, trying to be the best and trying to overtake everybody, to develop relationship with others.

Greatness is good only if it promotes the kingdom of God. God told Abraham that He would make his name great. Abraham became great for a good cause - he was blessed and in him all the families of the earth were blessed.

'And seekest thou great things for thyself? Seek them not for, behold I will bring evil upon all flesh, saith the LORD: but thy life will I give

unto thee for a prey in all places wither thou goest.' Jer. 45:5

Attainment of greatness does not exclude one from the challenges of life. Sometimes we may all of a sudden be surrounded by crisis situations. If all we do is surround ourselves with great things we will find out that there is no one to stand with us in times of difficulty.

Jesus elaborated on the need for relationship in his story of the unjust steward.

> *'And the lord commended the unjust steward, because he had done wisely: for the children of this world are in their generation wiser than the children of light. And I say unto you, make to yourselves friends of the mammon of unrighteousness; that, when ye fail, hey may receive you into everlasting habitations.'* Luke 16:8, 9

Note that Jesus did not commend that unjust steward; it was his master or lord who commended. The unjust steward had called his master's debtors and reduced their indebtedness in order to gain favor with them afterwards.

This unjust steward was in a position of responsibility. He could foresee the evil day ahead of him. He therefore made friends with his masters debtors. He knew that his authority (success) was temporary so he made an arrangement to be received into everlasting habitations.

This dishonest manager was likely to have added extra money to the indebtedness of his master's debtors with the hope of taking the extra for himself. When he realized he was going to lose his job he called the debtors and took of the extra he hoped to gain.

His master did not commend him for his dishonesty but for his foresight in preparing for his future mishap. The manager lost money in order to gain relationship. Jesus therefore admonished His listeners to make friends by giving away worldly goods.

The great lesson here is that it will cost us everything to make friends. It will cost us time. We will have to sacrifice our personal interest. We may have to spend our money on others. In a world, which is largely controlled by money, we must be careful not to be so greedy for money that we lose all our relationship.

The dishonest manager knew that when money is gone and a job is lost the only thing left is relationship with other people.

Jonathan had a healthy relationship with David. When Jonathan died, David showed kindness to Jonathan's son Mephibosheth. Your friends will share your fears with you.

In the time of your peace and prosperity invest in relationship, else in the time of war no one will come to your aid.

Most anointed people want to do things alone. They feel so powerful that they want to live on an island all by themselves. Samson walked alone and got himself into trouble.

Sometimes we think that it is the weak who need relationship. Most great folks therefore sit down waiting for the weak to come and seek relationship with them. That kind of relationship does not work. Relationship eliminates pride and a feeling of superiority. Mephibosheth ate from David's table. The great person, knowing the value of relationship, must do everything in his power to develop relationships with people God gives to him.

There is a tendency for great people to form a clique and seek to crush the weak. This is not relationship, but conspiracy. We must not relate based on what we possess. If two people relate because they both have good homes, good cars, large congregations, successful businesses and great academic qualifications, it is not good enough. If one of them loses what he has the relationship would be gone.

Since relationship is the key to lasting greatness, relationship with others will be severely tested. In view of this, we must resolve to make relationships that will last.

We will have to leave the comfort of our own success to relate to others outside what we call our own. The wisdom here is that if crisis hit you, your ministry suffers with you. It cannot lift you up. If you however relate to others, when you're hit they will be there to lift you up.

Any time you're standing when a brother is going down it is not an opportunity for you to boast in how strong you are. God allowed you to be standing at that moment so that you can lift the falling brother up.

Chapter 5

CONCERNING YOUR RIGHTS

A great man is entitled to many rights. He is entitled to respect, honor and material provision. Under certain conditions one may use all of his rights without jeopardizing his future. There are however, times when one cannot insist on ones rights. If he does, his system will explode or collapse.

Nehemiah is a typical example of a great man who refused to demand all his rights.

> 'Moreover from the time that I was appointed to be their governor in the land of Judah, from the twentieth year even unto the two and thirtieth year of Artaxerxes the King, that is, twelve years, I and my brethren have not eaten the dread of the governor.
>
> But the former governor that had been before me were chargeable unto the people, and had taken of them bread and wine, beside forty shekels of silver, yea, even their ser-

vants dare rule over the people but so did not!' 'because of the fear of God.'   Neh. 5:14, 15

This portion of scripture must cause the average twentieth century great man to bow his head in shame. For twelve years Nehemiah did not live on the right allowances and provisions of a governor. He was so burdened by the deplorable state of the walls of Jerusalem, which were broken down and burnt, that he could not satisfy any lust for food, power and money.

A great man must be so passionate about his environment and the people around him that he intentionally trims down his rights. Nehemiah did this for twelve years.

When a young man goes about claiming all of his rights in the ministry even before his work is established, he is heading for danger. To insist on unrealistic wages, a big house and a good car when your ministry or business is young, is dangerous.

We have defined greatness so wrongly that many people have placed their focus on the wrong things. They would therefore squeeze everybody and manipulate situations in order to get what they want.

Nehemiah decided to be different. You can choose to be different in this generation. Place others above achievements. Use achievements to bless others instead of using others just to attain your achievements. Nehemiah did not only check himself, he also checked his brothers who were co-workers with him. You can-

Concerning Your Rights

not claim to be great if you're straight and the people who surround you are all crooked.

There is nothing wrong with enjoying your rights when prevailing conditions in your business or family are good. But to claim these things at the wrong time is bad.

Jesus Christ though equal with God did not claim equality with the Father. If He had done so He couldn't have submitted Himself to come in the flesh, bear our sins and die on the cross. There are certain sacrifices we cannot make if we claim all of our rights.

Don't get offended when people refuse to honor you. How will you react if your wife, children or subordinates at work refused to honor you? Haman reacted wrongly when Mordecai refused to honor him.

> *'And when Haman saw that Mordecai bowed not, nor did him reverence, then was Haman full of wrath. And he thought scorn to lay hands on Mordecai alone;'*
> Esther 3:5, 6a

Haman was angry because he was not respected. Later he hanged himself to death. If all you do is focus on your rights, you will soon stop focusing on pleasing God.

Anyone who truly wants to be great must know this–greatness and greed don't go together.

Sometimes you see a man who finds a new job and spends all his time trying to figure out what's in the job for him. It is not wrong to know one's wages, but it is wrong to place wages above one's fulfillment in the job.

Young people go into the ministry and their ambition is to become great at once. They want big love offerings; they want all the benefits of senior ministers. Such people soon find out that a good name is better than wealth and power.

'A GOOD name is rather to be chosen than great riches, and loving favor rather than silver and gold.'
Prov. 22:1

We must learn to be sensitive to the plight of others in our quest to accomplish great things. Don't neglect others on your way up and don't hurt others in order to rise to the top.

Chapter 6

HONOR TO WHOM HONOR IS DUE

While the great amongst us must not compel us to honor them, it is both natural and spiritual for us to honor people upon whom God has bestowed greatness.

To acknowledge the greatness of a man whom God has made great is to surrender to the sovereignty of God. Sometimes we look at the background of someone and refuse to acknowledge his present status. At times we also allow our personal misgivings about the great person to hinder us from accepting him.

'Render therefore to all their dues: tribute to whom tribute is due; custom to whom custom; fear to who fear; honor to whom honor.

> *Owe no man any thing, but to love one another for he that loveth another hath fulfilled the law.'*
> Rom. 1:7, 8

If we refuse to honor the great ones amongst us we are doing injustice to God's system. Fathers deserve honor. Our bosses, spiritual leaders, husbands and leaders in secular authority deserve honor. Anyone who has refused to honor someone God has raised is actually in debt. We ought to owe no man anything but to love one another.

The principal key to honor is love. Love covers a multitude of wrong done against it and goes ahead to honor deserving fellows.

Love is patient. It does not hurry to be exalted so it gives honor to deserving fellows while it waits its turn. Impatience causes everyone to desire to be on top of the world at the same time.

Love is kind. Love is not callous. It will not use other people for selfish ambition. True greatness is attained without using human beings as objects of achievement.

Love does not envy. In most societies where people are striving for greatness it is common to see jealousy and strife amongst people. We can be great without destroying others. Ambitious people often destroy those ahead of them with certain accusations only to end up doing the same things they criticized. It is not wise to criticize what you don't understand. You cannot understand a situation or the implications of a position unless you've been there.

Love is not boastful. Don't be loud about anything.

Honor to Whom Honor is Due

Whosoever boasteth himself of a false gift is like clouds and wind without rain.' Prov. 25:24

When a man begins to draw the attention of people to something he does not really possess, he causes pain to the people. When we are just beginning to break through, our words must be few. Otherwise people will build their lives around us only to realize that we don't have what it takes to sustain our progress.

Love is not proud. True greatness is devoid of pride. Pride refuses correction. Greatness seeks every opportunity to be corrected. When prophet Nathan rebuked king David, he readily repented. Other kings resisted correction and were destroyed.

Greatness does not conduct itself badly. Love does not put others down. A great man must necessarily be a gentleman. Watch the way you talk to your wife and subordinates. Respect pedestrians and other road users whose vehicles may not be as posh as yours.

Love does not seek her own interest to the detriment of others. It is not easily provoked and does not conceive evil things about others.

Greatness is founded upon principles of righteousness. Love does not rejoice in acts of unrighteousness. Greatness bears every form of maltreatment until God releases it to manifest itself. If one cannot bear undermining, insults and cheating, one cannot be great. People are going to use you and refuse to appreciate you. You must be able to bear it.

The Price of Greatness

If you are to be great, you will have to learn to trust people. A suspicious and over cautious person cannot be great. Greatness always hopes to shine one day for that matter it endures all things.

Love never fails. David was great. He loved Saul to the end. Saul was envious of him but he remained respectful to Saul. Saul sought to kill him but he made a lamentation when Saul died. He did not rejoice in the death of Saul.

You may have good reasons to refuse to honor others but always remember that you will reap what you sow.

We honor others by giving them their due respect. We also honor our leaders by giving them our substances. The Bible enjoins us to honor our father and mother and if honoring the Lord with our substance is correct, then we ought to give to our parents.

One other way by which we honor the great people in our midst is to obey them and accept their corrections. They have walked in our paths before and it is worth listening to them.

We also honor the great by contributing to make them even greater. Add to the great man. Do not withhold from him. To him that has, more is added.

When the queen of Sheba saw the greatness of Solomon, she added wealth to him.

'And she said to the king, it was a true report which I heard in mine own land of thine acts, and of thy wisdom:

Howbeit I believed not their words, until I came, and mine eyes had seen it: and behold, the one half of the greatness of thy wisdom was not told me: for thou exceedest the fame that I heard.

Happy are thy men, and happy are these thy servants, which stand continually before thee, and hear thy wisdom.

Blessed be the Lord thy God, which delighted in thee to set thee on his throne, to be king for the LORD thy God; because thy God loved Israel, to establish them for ever, therefore made he thee king over them, to do judgment and justice.

And she gave the king an hundred and twenty talents of gold, and of spices great abundance, and precious stones: neither was there any such spice as the queen of Sheba gave king Solomon.' 2 Chron. 9:5-9

The queen of Sheba witnessed the greatness of Solomon. She added unto Solomon's greatness by giving him gold, spices and precious stones. She did not say he had more than enough. Sometimes we limit our miracle and blessing by withholding things from great people. There is a time to give to the needy out of compassion and there is a time to appreciate those who have affected your life in any way.

Greatness comes from God and when we honor it, we are acknowledging an act of God. One secret to receiving is sow not into a barren land, but in a fertile land. Sow in a blessed land.

Chapter 7

UNLIMITED GREATNESS

Greatness is a gift of God and since God cannot be limited, we cannot limit greatness. Greatness cannot be limited to a certain geographical region. God rules in the affairs of men everywhere and He is capable of raising a great man anywhere.

Time cannot also limit greatness. God raised great men in times of old and He is still raising them in our day. It is strange when people attribute the greatness of Isaac in the Bible to God and at the same time attribute the greatness of any modern day person to occultic powers.

These same people still confess that Jesus Christ is the same yesterday today and forever. We give the devil undue glory when we attribute the greatness of God's people to him.

Time and space don't limit greatness. Again greatness from God transcends all our imagination.

> *'Now unto him that is able to do exceeding abundantly above all that we ask or think, according to the power that worketh in us,'*   Eph. 3:20

God has deposited in us a potential for mind-blowing feats. This power lies within us and it is waiting to be released. Your mind cannot imagine what you're capable of being, unless God opens your eyes to see.

I have heard people say that the sky is the limit, but I tell you that God is the limit and since He is beyond comprehension, your greatness is limitless.

God asked Abraham to count the stars of heaven, but he could not, because they were uncountable. Then God said his seed would be as countless as the stars.

> *'Yea, they turned back and tempted God, and limited the Holy one of Israel.'*   Psalm 78:41

To limit God is to turn back. When I say, this is what God will do, and no more, I am limiting God. God is a Spirit. The wind blows where it wants and we cannot tell where it is going. Jealousy and unbelief may make us feel that what we have is of God but another person's is not.

The Bible says, if the Lord is our Shepherd, our cups will run over. It says that goodness and mercy will follow us all the days of our lives. We cannot stop God at a point.

Circumstances, demons and people can't stop your progress in greatness. Isaac increased in greatness. The

Unlimited Greatness

famine in the land and the opposition of the people there could not stop him.

'Then Isaac sowed in that land, and received in the same year an hundredfold: and the LORD blessed him.

And the man waxed great, and went forward, and grew until he became very great:

For he had possession of flocks, and possession of herds, and great store of servants: and the Philistines envied him.' Gen. 26:12-14

Greatness is progressive. It just keeps coming once you hit the road. The only thing that will take you backwards is when you miss out on God. Isaac waxed great; he went forward and grew until he was very great.

The Philistines envied him but that didn't stop him. They blocked the wells, which his father Abraham had dug and he went ahead and opened them, again.

Greatness defies opposition. Your greatness exposes the laziness, the weakness and incompetence of someone next door. He has always lived his life of mediocrity with the excuse that conditions are not favorable. Here you are, dismantling his hypothesis. He will naturally rise against you.

It is God's will for you to keep rising, but it is the wish of men to bring you down. Men may detract you if you spend all your time fighting them. Isaac did not concentrate on his detractors. He just went ahead and dug up the wells again. Go ahead and do likewise.

The growth of Isaac in greatness is a caution to those of us who see just a little success and believe that we have arrived. God gives us greatness so that by that greatness, we will get the entire world won to Jesus. Until this goal is achieved we cannot stop growing in greatness.

Chapter 8

THE CHALLENGES OF GREATNESS

Greatness attracts people to itself and that is where the greatest challenge is. Greatness attracts all kinds of people. It attracts your enemies to attack you. It attracts your friends to admire you. It also attracts some people to attach themselves to you and feed on your greatness.

Jesus illustrated this situation in a parable.

'Another parable put he forth unto them, saying, The kingdom of heaven is like to a grain of mustard seed, which a man too, and sowed in his field

Which indeed is the least of all seeds: but when it is grown, it is the greatest among herbs, and becometh a tree, so that the birds of the air come and lodge in the branches thereof.'   Matt 13:31, 32

The Price of Greatness

Greatness may begin from a mustard seed level and grow to become very big. Once it is grown the birds of the air will be attracted to it. Some of these birds come for shade; others come to attack the leaves and the fruit of the tree. Motives for settling on the tree are mixed.

Every great man must be wary of this. Some of the birds that came to lodge on the mustard tree could have been birds, which attempted to destroy the seed before it matured.

Joseph was sold into slavery in Egypt by his brothers. After many trials he became father to Pharaoh, the lord of Pharaoh's house and the ruler of the land of Egypt. His brothers came to Egypt and offered to be his servants and asked for his forgiveness. Joseph readily forgave them and assured them that God sent him ahead of them to preserve them. Great men must learn to forgive and reach out to people who persecute them, but later come back in repentance.

Greatness also attracts us to people who would come to test us. Many people don't really believe that one can be genuinely great in our time. His greatness is either attributed to demonic powers or dubious means. Others cannot believe that the great man is as great as the world portrays him to be. These people will therefore come around to test the great man in various ways. They will tempt him, entice him, lure him and feign need to see if he has what it takes to handle these. The queen of Sheba tested Solomon with hard questions.

Once we're great we must believe God for the wisdom to handle the queen of Sheba. We must trust God

The Challenges of Greatness

to deal with Satan as Christ dealt with him in the temptation in the wilderness.

Great people are daily confronted with the pressure to perform. A standard is set and people expect you to deliver the goods all the time. A truly great person knows his season. Jesus refused to submit to pressure. He refused to turn stone into bread. When He was confronted at the wedding to do something about a shortage of wine, He said His hour was not yet. He later turned water into wine when the right time struck.

If a great man does not resist being pushed by people, he will soon be overtaken by pretense, exaggeration, lying and cheating.

Greatness will also bring into your life people who just want to use you to achieve their goals and later on push you aside. They will use all kinds of flattering words on you just to lure you to give them credibility and recognition. Some of them will come around to steal some ideas from you only to develop them later and enter into competition with you.

A great person cannot stand as an island but he must learn to relate to people in wisdom, being as harmless as a dove, but at the same time, as wise as a serpent.

Like a swarm of flies some people will come against you with their hearts full of hatred and bitterness. They will do everything in their power to destroy. They will misrepresent you and set you up. The great person must be able to go forward without concentrating on his detractors. If you want to play their game and speak

The Price of Greatness

their language you will soon have their situation - you will be like them. They are the failures that they are, because they talk about things, which are not important, and they concentrate on the wrong things.

One other challenge of a great man is that he will by nature breed and reproduce other great people. Greatness begets greatness. Some of the great people he begets will acknowledge him and honor - him. Others will deny him his due honor. While some of the great people are with him they will develop their independent ways of thinking and doing things. David had Joab to handle. Joab had his own style. A great person is one who is master in handling things like this.

The challenges, fears, uncertainties, and inconveniences of greatness can be extremely uncomfortable.

Let us consider those who will come to greatness because of genuine need. Everybody goes to the great man believing that he has what it takes to meet his or her need. If he fails to help he is either considered to be weak, selfish or indifferent. The great person will have to be at peace with his God and with his conscience in this matter. Always remember that you cannot do everything for everybody all of the time. Do what God enables you to do at any given time and stop there. Be frank with people. Don't make promises you cannot fulfill.

Chapter 9

PRESERVING GREATNESS

It is our duty to preserve greatness. Greatness is a rare virtue in a generation, which underutilizes the grace of God. Few people are able to utilize the seed of grace to produce greatness. Indeed, many are called but few are chosen.

We are stewards of the gifts and talents of God. Great people are gifts from God to brighten this dark world where mediocrity is the accepted norm.

Great people must be cautious not to destroy themselves through personal negligence. Those who are supposed to be beneficiaries of greatness must not be moved by ignorance and jealousy to kill it.

David's men saw his greatness and sought to preserve it. In a war against the Philistines, David nearly lost his life. When it was time to fight against the mischievous Absalom, David's men restrained him from going to battle.

'But the people answered, thou shalt not go forth: for if we flee away, they will not care for us; neither if half of us die, will they care for us: but now thou art

The Price of Greatness

worth ten thousand of us: therefore now it is better that thou, succor us out of the city. II Sam. 18:3

We preserve greatness by restraining it from endangering itself. Don't insist that the great man must engage in every activity in the community. There are times we must exclude some people from certain things just so that they can live longer and be a blessing to us.

Privileges given to the great people amongst us must be seen as benefiting everyone ultimately. Sometimes these great people have gone through the toils and hazards of life so often that they are now virtually weak. We demonstrate our maturity when we don't insist that they must be like us in all things.

It is interesting to see David's people equate him to ten thousand of them. They saw his worth. This attitude of theirs explains why David was so influential in their lives. Unless you have a revelation of a person's value he cannot be a blessing to you.

It is amazing how the body of Christ kills great people amongst them and then turn around to pray that God should give therm great men.

'For he that hath, to him shall be given: and he that hath not, from him shall be taken even that which he hath.'   Mark 4:25

This statement of Jesus means that anyone who has anything and uses it well, there is a promise by God that more will be added to him until he has much. But anyone who has little and does not use it properly even the little he has will be taken away from him.

The imperfections of a great person must not be used to destroy him.

Preserving Greatness

Our attitude towards the great ones amongst us must not always be negative. Sometimes we don't destroy directly through negative pronouncement or thoughts, but through neglect. We tend to believe that we need these great people but we seldom believe that they need us too. As we take interest in great people and make inputs into their lives we preserve them in a direct way.

Chapter 10

EBENEZER

It is God who gives greatness and we must give Him the glory for our state of elevation. This assertion is so often talked about that I may bore readers by elaborating on it. There is however no harm in reminding us about something we are already familiar with.

The word Ebenezer appears in the Bible when Israel defeated the Philistines in a battle.

'And the men of Israel went out of Mizpeh, and pursued the Philistines, and smote them, until they came under Bethcar. Then Samuel took a stone, and set it between Mizpeh and Shen, and called the name of it Ebenezer, saying, hitherto hath the LORD helped us.'
I Sam. 7:11, 12

God gave Israel victory in the battle and Samuel clearly attributed all the glory to God by naming the place Ebenezer - thus far has God brought us. This must be the confession of every great man.

The Price of Greatness

The ultimate glory of our greatness must be to God. Nothing done in the power of the flesh glorifies God. Most great people can easily trace their beginning to a humble point in a certain sense. Some begin life with a poor level of intelligence; others with a financially poor status and others begin their walk with God from a background of spiritual darkness.

I clearly remember from where the Lord took me. It is good for a man to constantly remember where he came from. It helps one to remain humble, and it also allows for total dependence on God. The blessings of God in my life are no secret. I can confidently say that I am a living testimony of the faithfulness of God.

'For ye see your calling, brethren, how that not many wise men after the flesh, not many mighty, not many noble, are called:

But God hath chosen the foolish things of the world to confound the wise; and God hath chosen the weak things of the world to confound the things, which are mighty;

And the base things of the world, and things which are despised, hath God chosen, yea, and things which are not, to bring to naught things that are: That no flesh should glory in his presence.'   *I Cor. 1:26-29*

To forget where one comes from is a very unfortunate condition. Many people who do this are soon overtaken by pride and God rejects them.

In order to reach our point of greatness with a conscience that can give glory to God, we must be mindful about how we attain our goals.

We must not attain our status by fraud; least our conscience condemns us. To pull others down in order to rise in life is evil. Bribery and the use of gifts and money to sway judgment in our favor is also evil.

We live in a time when non-Christians are gradually infiltrating the Church. They know that money and material things are needed to build God's kingdom. They therefore come giving out money to the Church, but not their hearts to God. People who would be made great by God must turn down such gifts and support from evil men who have no genuine heart but seek to manipulate the power of God in the Church. Abraham refused the, gifts of the king of Sodom.

'And the king of Sodom said unto Abram, Give me the persons and take the goods to thyself

And Abram said to the king of Sodom, I have lift up mine hand unto the LORD, the most high God, the possessor of heaven and earth,

> *That I will not take from a thread even to a shoe latchet, and that I will not take anything that is thine, lest thou shouldest say, I have made Abram rich:'*
> Gen. 14:21-23

It is obvious from the above scripture that Abraham had prayed earlier about the possibility of receiving gifts from the king of Sodom. He had prayed for victory in the battle and his motive for delivering the people of Sodom was pure.

If you don't pray about certain details you will become a prey to your adversaries. The Bible says that Abraham was rich in cattle in silver and in gold (Gen.

13:2). Contrary to most people who are supposedly great however, Abraham did not just go grabbing things from just anybody. God was actively involved in how he got to the top.

When our conscience is clear about the source of our greatness then and only then can we say 'Ebenezer.' When we acknowledge God in our greatness He keeps us there. We acknowledge Him when we maintain our fellowship with Him and involve Him through prayer and meditation in our daily walk. It is common to see people abandon God and resort to human wisdom once they attain greatness. The funny thing about such people is that, before God placed them where they are today, they were diligent in their quest to serve God. With a little success blowing their way, they become so busy chasing after money and business connections that it stifles their desire to serve God.

Greatness comes from God and is meant to glorify God and promote His kingdom. As you come to the end of this book determine to seek God and not great things for yourself. The goods of this world and the celebrity status the world bestows on people will all pass away. Love never fails. In everything therefore our love for God and humanity must supersede every other thing. Amen.

Process is Designed for Purpose

Process is Designed for Purpose

The Price of Greatness